21-Day Weight Gain Meal Plan

The ultimate 3-week guide to help you gain weight and improve your body functions.

Barbara T. Davies

Disclaimer

This book is meant as a valuable source of information, and not intended as a substitute for consultation with a licensed practitioner. Please consult with your own physician or healthcare specialist regarding the suggestions and recommendations made in this book. The use of this book implies your acceptance of this disclaimer.

The publisher and the author make no guarantees concerning the level of success you may experience by following the advice and strategies contained in this book, and you accept the risk that results will differ for each individual.

The publisher and the author disclaim all such representations and warranties, including but not limited to warranties of healthcare for a particular purpose. In addition, the publisher and the author assume no responsibility for errors, inaccuracies, omissions, or any other inconsistencies herein.

Copyright © Barbara T. Davies

All rights reserved. No part of this publication may be reproduced in any form or by any means, including scanning, photocopying or otherwise without prior written permission of the copyright holder.

Table Of Contents

Disclaimer	2
How to calculate your calorie requirement?	5
How do I use this meal plan?	7
WEEK 1	9
WEEK 1 SMOOTHIE RECIPES	12
WEEK 1 MAIN RECIPES	17
WEEK 1 GROCERY LIST	35
WEEK 2	37
WEEK 2 SMOOTHIE RECIPES	40
WEEK 2 MAIN RECIPES	44
WEEK 2 GROCERY LIST	56
WEEK 3	59
WEEK 3 SMOOTHIE RECIPES	62

WEEK 3 MAIN MEALS	**65**
WEEK 3 GROCERY LIST	**78**
NOTE	**80**
SNACK SUGGESTIONS	**82**
FROM THE AUTHOR	**84**

How to calculate your calorie requirement?

Eating random calories will not serve you to gain healthy weight. How many calories you need depends on your height, weight and BMR along with your activity level.

How Many Calories Do I Need To Gain Weight?

The more you expend in exercise the more you need to consume. Adding 500 calories a day helps to gain 250-500 gm per week or 1lb, a standard way to gain weight. If you want fast weight gain then adding 700-1000 calories per day should help you gain 1kg per week.

Calculate your required calories with MyFitnessPal, lifesum or any online calculator..

You should follow up with your preferred calculator every two to three weeks as your weight gradually increases, causing changes in your calorie requirements.

After attaining your desired weight, you could also employ the use of a calculator to determine your weight maintenance calorie requirements.

How do I use this meal plan?

☐ There are four meals per day (breakfast, lunch, dinner and a smoothie), totalling to **3100-3400** calories daily.

☐ Feel free to break up your meals into 5-6 meals if you can't stomach the 4 meals per day. A tip is to eat every 2-3 hours. Start eating early.

☐ This meal plan is designed for one person. If you would like to use them for multiple people, simply multiply the ingredients quantities by the total number of people.

☐ There are smoothie recipes for each week, and you are expected to pick any to consume daily as a snack. Protein powders are not included in the smoothie recipes but feel free to include your protein powder in any of the smoothies, or take your powder separately with milk or water.

- There are included snack suggestions at the end of the book. Feel free to add them to your daily menu but don't feel pressured to, because the four initial meals already surpass 3000 calories.

- **Be flexible!** Feel free to replace any of the ingredients or recipes with *your* personal choices and adjust ingredient amounts to fit your macros and situation.

- Weekly grocery lists are included to keep you organized.

- If you follow a very **strict** diet, make sure to personalize this meal plan to make it work for you.

WEEK 1

	BREAKFAST	LUNCH
SUNDAY	Strawberry Vanilla Pancakes Calories: 765cal.	Oven-Roasted Sweet Potatoes Calories:800cal
MONDAY	Omelet: 2 large eggs, 1 tbsp butter, 2 tbsp grated cheese, cherry tomatoes, herbs and spices of choice. Oatmeal: ½ cup raw quick oats, 1 cup whole milk, 1 medium banana, cinnamon, sweetener of choice. Calories:780cal	Grilled chicken sandwich: 4oz grilled chicken, 2 slices cheese, lettuce, tomato, 1 tbsp mayonnaise, 2 slices whole wheat bread 1 medium apple + 2tbsp peanut butter Calories:870cal
TUESDAY	French toast + 1 medium banana Calories:830cal	Leftover fried spaghetti Calories:765cal
WEDNESDAY	Peanut butter and strawberry jelly oatmeal Calories:710cal	1st portion Egg-fried rice Calories:725cal
THURSDAY	Banana chocolate chip pancakes Calories:940cal	Chicken sweet potatoes hash Calories:820cal

FRIDAY	French toast + 1 medium banana Calories:830cal	1st portion fried spaghetti Calories:765cal
SATURDAY	Almond joy oatmeal & 1 medium apple + 2tbsp peanut butter Calories:825cal	Omelet: 3 large eggs, 1 tbsp butter, 2 tbsp grated cheese, cherry tomatoes, herbs and spices of choice. 2 slices whole wheat toast 1 tbsp butter 1 medium banana Calories:715cal

	DINNER	SMOOTHIE	TOTAL CALORIES
SUNDAY	Peanut butter and banana sandwich: 2 slices bread toast, 4 tbsp peanut butter, 1 medium banana, 1 cup whole milk Calories:756cal	✓	3,121 cal.
MONDAY	1st portion fried spaghetti Calories:765cal	✓	3,215 cal.
TUESDAY	Chicken sweet potatoes hash Calories:820cal	✓	3,215 cal.

WEDNESDAY	Grilled chicken sandwich & 1 medium apple + 2tbsp peanut butter **Calories:870cal**	✓	3,105 cal.
THURSDAY	Leftover fried rice **Calories:725cal**	✓	3,285 cal.
FRIDAY	Mayo chicken sandwich **Calories:770cal**	✓	3,165 cal.
SATURDAY	Leftover fried spaghetti **Calories:765cal**	✓	3,105 cal.

WEEK 1 SMOOTHIE RECIPES

MANGO BANANA SMOOTHIE

Calories: 800cal.

Prep Time: 3 mins.
Cook Time: 2 mins.

INGREDIENTS:

- ☐ 2 fresh mangoes or 2 cups of frozen mango.
- ☐ 1 small frozen banana. You can use unfrozen if you use frozen mango.
- ☐ 1 cup whole milk.
- ☐ ½ cup nonfat plain Greek yogurt.
- ☐ 1-2 tablespoon(s) honey.

DIRECTIONS:

Add all ingredients to a high-powered blender and blend until creamy. Feel free to add more milk if it is too thick.

+ A 250cal GRANOLA BAR (the smoothie itself is 550cal).

CASHEW DATE SHAKE

Calories: 810cal.

Prep Time: 2hrs.
Cook Time: 2 mins.

INGREDIENTS:

- ½ cup raw cashews, soaked for 2-4hrs.
- 4-5 Medjool dates, soaked for 10 minutes.
- 1 medium banana, sliced and optionally frozen.
- ½ cup whole milk.
- 1 ½ cups of ice.

- ¾ teaspoon vanilla extract.
- Pinch of nutmeg.
- Pinch cinnamon.
- Pinch of salt.

DIRECTIONS:

Add your soaked and drained cashews and dates to a high-powered blender. Add the remaining ingredients and blend on high until thick and creamy.

STRAWBERRY GREEK YOGURT SMOOTHIE

Calories: 800cal.

Prep Time: 3 mins.
Cook Time: 2 mins.

INGREDIENTS:

- 1 ½ frozen strawberries.

- 1 medium ripe banana.
- 1 cup nonfat plain Greek yogurt.
- 4 tablespoons oatmeal.
- 2 ½ tablespoons peanut butter.
- 1 tablespoon honey.
- 1 cup whole milk, ice(optional).

DIRECTIONS:

- Place all of the ingredients but the ice in a blender.
- Blend until smooth. If the mixture is too thick to blend, splash in more milk, stir to move the contents of the blender around, and blend again; if it is too thin, blend in a few ice cubes. Taste and add additional honey if you would like the smoothie sweeter.

AVOCADO CHOCOLATE SMOOTHIE BOWL

Calories: 850cal.

Prep Time: 4 mins.
Cook Time: 2 mins.

INGREDIENTS:

- 2 cups whole milk.
- ½ avocado (100g).
- 1 medium ripe banana.
- 2 tablespoons peanut butter.
- 1 tablespoon cocoa powder.
- 1 tablespoon ground flaxseed or chia seed.
- 2-3 dates or 2-3 tablespoons of honey.
- 1 cup ice.

DIRECTIONS:

Combine all ingredients in a blender and blend until smooth. Add more honey to taste if desired. Add toppings of your choice such as granola, chocolate chips, nuts, seeds, shredded coconut, fruit slices.

WEEK 1 MAIN RECIPES

STRAWBERRY VANILLA PANCAKES

Calories: 765cal.

Prep Time: 6 mins.
Cook Time: 15 mins.

INGREDIENTS:

- 1 cup + 2 tbsp all purpose flour.
- 3 tbsps sugar.
- ¾ tablespoon baking powder.
- Pinch of salt.
- 2 ¼ tablespoons butter.
- 1 cup milk.
- 1 ½ teaspoon vanilla extract.
- 1 egg.
- ¾ cup strawberries.

DIRECTIONS:

Batter:
- Whisk together the dry ingredients. (flour, baking powder, sugar, and salt).
- Melt the butter. You can do this in a big microwave-proof bowl or jug, that's large enough to hold all the wet ingredients to reduce dirty dishes.
- Whisk together the wet ingredients (melted butter, egg, vanilla, milk).
- Add the wet ingredients to the dry ingredients, whisk them until well combined. Don't worry about a few lumps.
- Leave the batter to rest for 10 mins.
- While the batter is resting, dice the strawberries into cubes.
- Fold the diced strawberries into the pancake batter.

Cook the pancakes:
- Heat a pan to medium heat, make sure it has a nice flat base.
- Add a little butter or oil to the surface of the pan.
- Scoop the desired quantity of the batter (about 1/4cup for mini pancakes) and pour it onto the heated pan. Your pancake won't be perfectly round due to the strawberry lumps, so don't worry about the imperfect circles.
- Watch for small bubbles to appear on the surface of the pancake and burst, when you see them, it's time to flip the pancake.
- The second side of the pancake won't take long to cook, watch the edges of the pancake and check for bubbles appearing and you will be able to see when the center of the pancake is cooked.

OVEN-ROASTED SWEET POTATOES

Calories: 800cal.

Prep Time: 10 mins.
Cook Time: 30 mins.

INGREDIENTS:

- 2 pounds sweet potatoes.
- 2 tablespoons of olive oil.
- ½- ¾ teaspoon salt.
- ¼ teaspoon garlic powder.
- ¼ teaspoon black pepper.
- ½-¾ teaspoon smoked paprika.

DIRECTIONS:

- Trim the ends of the sweet potatoes, peel, and cut into cubes.
- Put the potatoes in a large bowl, add the oil, garlic powder, black pepper, paprika, and salt. Toss until the potatoes are well coated.
- Lightly spray a baking sheet with cooking oil spray. Arrange the sweet potatoes on the baking sheet in one single layer and spread evenly to prevent sticking.

- Place in the center rack of a 425ºF (220°C) preheated oven and bake for 30 to 40 minutes or till the sweet potatoes become fork tender. (Flip every 10 minutes)Sprinkle over with chopped parsley and serve immediately.

FRIED SPAGHETTI

Calories: 1530cal.

Prep Time: 5 mins.
Cook Time: 15 mins.

INGREDIENTS:

- 250g spaghetti.
- ¾ cup sliced mixed peppers (red, yellow, green).
- ¾ cup mixed vegetables (sweet corn, peas and other veggies of choice).
- 150g shrimp.
- ½ medium onion, chopped.
- 1 clove garlic, minced.

☐ 0.5 teaspoon black pepper.

- 1 ½ tablespoons soy sauce.
- 0.5 teaspoon thyme powder.
- 0.5 teaspoon curry powder.
- 2 tablespoons vegetable oil.
- 2 tablespoons of spring onions, *chopped*.
- salt to taste.
- ½ a seasoning cube.

DIRECTIONS:

- Add water in a pot and put on your gas. Add a tablespoon of vegetable oil and leave to boil before adding salt and spaghetti.
- Cook for 15 minutes or till spaghetti is cooked al dente. Drain and set aside.
- Put a wok or pan on your gas, put in the remaining vegetable oil and add the shrimps.
- Fry the shrimps for 3 minutes before adding garlic, onions, mixed vegetables, mixed peppers and spring onions.
- Add seasoning cube(s), curry powder, dried thyme and soy sauce then add in the cooked spaghetti.
- Stir and mix well before taking off the heat.

This recipe is for two portions, so divide into two parts, eat one and refrigerate the leftover in a sealed container for the next day.

FRENCH TOAST

Calories: 730cal.

Prep Time: 5 mins.
Cook Time: 15 mins.

INGREDIENTS:

- 2 large eggs.
- ½ cup whole milk.
- 5 slices of bread (better if slightly stale).
- 1 tsp cinnamon.
- 1 tbsp butter.
- 2 tbsps maple syrup or honey.
- fresh berries (optional).
- 1 tsp freshly grated orange zest (optional).
- Whipped cream, apple butter, powdered sugar, chocolate chips (optional).

DIRECTIONS:

- In a bowl, whisk together the eggs, milk, and cinnamon. Stir in the orange zest if using. Whisk the mixture until well blended and pour into a shallow bowl, wide enough to place a slice of the bread you will be using.

- Place each slice of bread into the milk egg mixture, allowing the bread to soak in some of it.
- Melt butter in a large skillet over medium high heat. Shake off the excess egg mixture from the bread and place the bread slices onto the hot skillet. Fry the French toast until browned on one side, then flip and brown the other side.
- Serve the French toast hot with maple syrup or honey and/or with any of your other preferred toppings.

CHICKEN SWEET POTATOES HASH

Calories: 820cal.

Prep Time: 10 mins.
Cook Time: 15 mins.

INGREDIENTS:

For the Ground Chicken:
- 1 tbsp olive oil.
- ¼ onion chopped.

- ☐ ½ lb ground chicken.
- ☐ ¼ tsp cayenne pepper.
- ☐ 1 tsp smoked paprika.
- ☐ ¼ tsp thyme.
- ☐ salt to taste.
- ☐ black pepper to taste.
- ☐ 1 tbsp water if necessary.

For the Potatoes:
- ☐ 1 tbsp olive oil.
- ☐ 1.25 lb sweet potatoes peeled and cut into ½ inch cubes.
- ☐ ½ tsp paprika.
- ☐ Salt and pepper to taste.
- ☐ Black pepper to taste.
- ☐ ½ cup bell peppers red, yellow, green.
- ☐ 1-2 tbsp thinly sliced green onions (optional).

DIRECTIONS:

- ☐ Preheat two tablespoons of oil in a skillet on medium heat. Add the diced onions and cook until translucent for 1 to 2 minutes.
- ☐ Add the ground chicken and use a wooden spoon to break it into smaller pieces. Add cayenne pepper, paprika, thyme, salt, black pepper, and one tablespoon of water if necessary.
- ☐ Cook for another 5 minutes or until the meat is no longer pink. Remove from the pan and set it aside.
- ☐ Add two more tablespoons of oil to the same pan. Season the sweet potatoes with paprika, salt, and black pepper and add them to the

skillet. Stir frequently, about every 2 minutes, until potatoes are tender, about 10 to 12 minutes. You can add 1 to 2 tablespoons of oil, if needed, to prevent the sweet potatoes from burning.
- Stir in the bell pepper. Cook for another two minutes, then stir in the cooked ground chicken.
- Sprinkle some green onions, parsley, or cilantro over it if desired, and serve hot.

PEANUT BUTTER AND STRAWBERRY JELLY OATMEAL

Calories: 710cal.

Prep Time: 3 mins.
Cook Time: 4 mins.

INGREDIENTS:
- ½ cup old fashioned rolled oats.
- 1 cup whole milk.
- 1/4 cup non-fat Greek yogurt.
- 1 tablespoon chia seeds.

- 1 tablespoon sweetener, honey or maple syrup.
- ¼ teaspoon vanilla extract.
- 1 ¼ tablespoons strawberry jam.
- 1 ¼ tablespoon peanut butter.
- 2 ½ tablespoons crushed peanuts.
- ¼ cup diced strawberries.

DIRECTIONS:

- Bring the cup of milk, sweetener of choice and vanilla extract to a boil in a small saucepan.
- Stir oats and reduce heat to medium; cook for 1 minute.
- Remove from heat and let stand for 2 minutes to cool off.
- Add yogurt, chia seeds, strawberry jam, peanut butter, crushed peanuts and diced strawberries as toppings.

EGG-FRIED RICE

Calories: 1450cal.

Prep Time: 5 mins.

Cook Time: **10 mins.**

INGREDIENTS:

- 2 ¼ tablespoons butter, *divided.*
- 2 large eggs, *whisked.*
- 1 ½ medium carrots, *peeled and diced.*
- 1 small white onion, *diced.*
- ¼ cup frozen peas.
- 2 ¼ cloves garlic, *minced.*
- Salt and black pepper to taste.
- 3 cups of cooked and chilled rice.
- 2 ¼ green onions, *thinly sliced.*
- 2 ¼ - 3 tablespoons soy sauce, or more to taste.
- 1.5 teaspoons oyster sauce (optional).
- ¼ teaspoons toasted sesame oil.

DIRECTIONS:

- Heat 1/2 tablespoon of butter in a large sauté pan* over medium-high heat until melted. Add egg, and cook until scrambled, stirring occasionally. Remove egg, and transfer to a separate plate.
- Add an additional 1 tablespoon butter to the pan and heat until melted. Add carrots, onion, peas and garlic, and season with salt and pepper. Sauté for about 5 minutes or until the onion and carrots are soft. Increase heat to high, add in the remaining 1 1/2 tablespoons of butter, and stir until melted.

- ☐ Immediately add the rice, green onions, soy sauce and oyster sauce (if using), and stir until combined.
- ☐ Continue sautéing for an additional 3 minutes to fry the rice, stirring occasionally. (let the rice rest for a bit between stirs so that it can crisp up on the bottom.)
- ☐ Then add in the eggs and stir to combine. Remove from heat, and stir in the sesame oil until combined. Taste and season with extra soy sauce, if needed.

This recipe is for two portions, so divide into two parts, eat one and refrigerate the leftover in a sealed container for the next day.

BANANA CHOCOLATE CHIP COOKIE PANCAKE

Calories: 940cal.

Prep Time: 6 mins.
Cook Time: 15 mins.

INGREDIENTS:

- ¾ cup all-purpose flour.
- 2 ½ tbsp sugar.
- ¾ tsp baking powder.
- ¼ tsp cinnamon.
- ¼ tsp salt.
- 1 tsp vanilla extract (optional).
- 1 ½ tablespoons butter.
- ¾ medium ripe banana, *mashed*.
- 2 large eggs.
- ½ cup whole milk.
- ¼ cup mini chocolate chips.

DIRECTIONS:

- Whisk the flour, sugar, baking powder, cinnamon, and salt together in a large bowl. Whisk the mashed banana, eggs, melted butter, vanilla if using, and milk together in a medium bowl and add to the dry ingredients. Stir gently until the ingredients are just combined. Fold in mini chocolate chips. The batter will be thick.
- Heat a large nonstick skillet over medium heat. Add a little butter or oil to the surface of the pan.
- Make mini pancakes, using about ¼ cup for each, cooking the pancakes until the outer edges firm up and the bottom is golden brown, about 1½ minutes. Flip and cook the other side until golden brown, another 1½ minutes.

- Transfer the pancakes to a plate and set aside. Serve with maple syrup, honey or chocolate syrup.

MAYO CHICKEN SANDWICH

Calories: 770cal.

Prep Time: 5 mins.
Cook Time: 10 mins.

INGREDIENTS:

- 3 slices of bread.
- ¾ cup chicken, *shredded*.
- 1 tsp butter for toasting bread.
- 1 tbsp olive oil.
- 1 tbsp minced garlic or 2 cloves.
- Generous pinch of paprika or red chili powder.
- Pinch of any spice powder (all spice or garam masala).
- 3 tbsps mayonnaise.
- ¼ tsp mustard powder (optional).

- ¼ tsp pepper of choice.
- Salt as needed.
- 3-4 tbsp onions or cucumber, chopped.
- Onion springs, cilantro or parsley finely chopped.

DIRECTIONS:

- Butter the bread slices and toast them on a griddle until golden. Set these aside.
- You can either boil the chicken or saute it in oil to give it a grilled flavor and taste.
- To saute , add some oil on the griddle and saute the garlic until it smells good.
- Saute chicken along with salt until done. Sprinkle the spice powders. Toss well. Switch off heat and cool off.
- Add pepper, mustard powder and mayo to a bowl. Mix everything well.
- Add in chopped onions and herbs. Mix and add in the chicken.

For the sandwich:

- Spoon the properly stirred chicken, herb and spices mixture over the toasted bread. Cover with another slice and press down.
- Halve the chicken sandwich and serve.

ALMOND JOY OATMEAL

Calories: 550cal.

Prep Time: 3 mins.
Cook Time: 4 mins.

INGREDIENTS:
- ½ cup old fashioned rolled oats.
- 1 cup whole milk.
- 1/4 cup non-fat Greek yogurt.
- ¼ cup shredded coconut.
- 1 tablespoon almonds, *chopped*.
- 1 tablespoon chocolate chips.
- 1 tablespoon chia seeds.
- 1 tablespoon sweetener, honey or maple syrup.
- ¼ teaspoon vanilla extract.

DIRECTIONS:
- Bring the cup of milk, sweetener of choice and vanilla extract to a boil in a small saucepan.
- Stir oats and reduce heat to medium; cook for 1 minute.

- Remove from heat and let stand for 2 minutes to cool off.
- Add yogurt, chia seeds, shredded coconut, chopped almonds, and chocolate chips as toppings.

BONUS SNACK RECIPE

PEAR CRISPS

Calories: 246cal per serving.

Prep Time: 15mins.
Cook Time: 50 mins.
Servings: 6.

INGREDIENTS:
FOR THE FILLING:
- 6 cups peeled and sliced pears (about 6-7 medium pears) (or use a combination of apples and pears).
- 1 teaspoon vanilla extract.
- 1 ½ teaspoons cinnamon.
- ¼ teaspoon of nutmeg.

- ¼ teaspoon salt.

FOR THE TOPPING:

- 1 stick (½ cup) salted butter, softened at room temperature.
- ½ cup all-purpose flour.
- ½ cup rolled oats.
- ½ cup granulated sugar.
- ½ cup brown sugar.
- ⅓ cup finely-chopped pecans.
- ¼ teaspoon salt.
- Optional, for serving: vanilla ice cream and caramel sauce.

DIRECTIONS:

- Preheat the oven to 350°F. Grease an 8-inch square baking dish.
- Place peeled, sliced pears in a large bowl. Add vanilla, cinnamon, nutmeg, and ¼ teaspoon salt; toss to coat.
- Transfer pears to the prepared baking dish.
- In a separate bowl, use a fork (or your fingers) to mix together butter, flour, oats, granulated sugar, brown sugar, pecans, and salt until completely combined. The mixture will be lumpy and clumpy and should look like a streusel crumb topping.
- Spread topping evenly over the pears.
- Sprinkle with more cinnamon, if desired.
- Bake for 45 minutes, or until the top becomes golden brown and crispy and the pears are soft. Remove from the oven and let cool for 5-10 minutes. Serve warm or at room temperature. Top with vanilla ice cream and caramel sauce!

WEEK 1 GROCERY LIST

VEGETABLES	MISC	DAIRY	BAKING
Corn: as desired	Rice: 3 cups, cooked	Butter: 11 tbsps	All-purpose flour: 2 cups
Carrots: 2, medium	Spaghetti: 250g	Milk: 6 cups, whole milk	Sugar
Peas: ¼ cup, frozen	Bread: 21 slices	Cheese of your choice: 4-5 slices	Baking powder
Onions: 3, medium	Oats:1 ½ cups, quick oats	Mayonnaise:4 tbsps	Vanilla extract
Spring onions: 2	Sweet Potatoes: 3.2Ib	Greek yogurt: ½ cup non-fat or full-fat	Maple syrup
Parsley or cilantro: as desired	Strawberry jam: 2 tbsps	**MISC**	Chocolate chips:½ cup
Cherry tomatoes: as desired	Peanut butter:11 tbsps	Cayenne pepper	Shredded coconut:¼ cup
Bell peppers: mixture, 1 cup	Chia seeds: 2 tbsps	Garlic powder	Cinnamon
Garlic: 6 cloves	Olive oil	Smoked paprika	Honey
Green onions: 3	Vegetable oil	Black pepper	

| Lettuce | Peanuts & almonds | Toasted sesame oil | |

FRUITS	PROTEIN	MISC
Apples: 3, medium	Shrimp: 150g	Soy sauce
Bananas: 5, medium	Egg:12, large	Salt
Strawberries:1 cup	Chicken: 8oz	Curry & thyme powder
	Chicken: ½ lb, ground	Seasoning cube

- ☐ Include the ingredients of your chosen smoothies for the week (just double or triple the ingredients). Remember to include your protein powder if you use them.
- ☐ Don't forget to include your snacks if you're getting any.

WEEK 2

	BREAKFAST	LUNCH
SUNDAY	Grilled chicken sandwich: 4oz grilled chicken, 2 slices cheese, lettuce, tomato, 1 tbsp mayonnaise, 2 slices whole wheat bread 1 medium apple + 2tbsp peanut butter <u>Calories:870cal</u>	1st portion of Rice and beans <u>Calories:800cal</u>
MONDAY	Assorted yogurt granola bowl <u>Calories:835cal</u>	Leftover pan-fried pepperoni pizza <u>Calories:815cal</u>
TUESDAY	French toast + 1 medium banana <u>Calories: 830cal</u>	Chicken Quesadilla <u>Calories:744cal</u>
WEDNESDAY	Peanut butter and strawberry jelly oatmeal <u>Calories:710cal</u>	1st portion of Spaghetti with beef sauce <u>Calories:972cal</u>
THURSDAY	Banana chocolate chip pancakes <u>Calories:940cal</u>	1st portion of Egg-fried rice <u>Calories:725cal</u>
FRIDAY	Assorted yogurt granola	Chicken Quesadilla

	bowl Calories:835cal	Calories:744cal
SATURDAY	Omelet: 3 large eggs, 1 tbsp butter, 2 tbsp grated cheese, cherry tomatoes, herbs and spices of choice. + 2 slices bread toast, 2 tbsp butter or nut butter, 1 medium apple Calories:800cal	Chicken sweet potatoes hash Calories:820cal

	DINNER	SMOOTHIE	TOTAL CALORIES
SUNDAY	1st portion of pan-fried pepperoni pizza Calories:815cal	✓	3,285cal
MONDAY	Omelet: 2 large eggs, 1 tbsp butter, 2 tbsp grated cheese, cherry tomatoes, herbs and spices of choice. Oatmeal: ½ cup raw quick oats, 1 cup whole milk, 1 medium banana, cinnamon, sweetener of choice. Calories:780cal	✓	3,235cal

TUESDAY	Leftover rice and beans <u>Calories:800cal</u>	✓	3,174cal
WEDNESDAY	Mayo chicken sandwich <u>Calories:770cal</u>	✓	3,252cal
THURSDAY	Leftover spaghetti with beef sauce <u>Calories:972cal</u>	✓	3,437cal
FRIDAY	Leftover Egg-fried rice <u>Calories:725cal</u>	✓	3,104cal
SATURDAY	Banana chocolate chip oatmeal <u>Calories:685cal</u>	✓	3,105cal

WEEK 2 SMOOTHIE RECIPES

CHOCOLATE PEANUT BUTTER SMOOTHIE

Calories: 800cal.

Prep Time: 3 mins.
Cook Time: 3 mins.

INGREDIENTS:

- ☐ 1 cup whole milk.
- ☐ ½ cup full fat Greek yogurt.
- ☐ 1 medium banana, preferably frozen.
- ☐ 1 tbsp coconut oil, melted or 2 ½ tbsp coconut flakes.

- ☐ 2 tbsps chia seeds or 1 tbsp flax, 1 tbsp chia.
- ☐ 1 tbsp dark cocoa powder.
- ☐ 2 tbsps peanut butter.
- ☐ 1 tsp vanilla extract.
- ☐ ¾ tbsp nutella or 1 tbsp chocolate syrup or 2 tbsps chocolate chips.

DIRECTIONS:

Add all ingredients to a high-powered blender and blend until creamy. Feel free to add more milk if it is too thick.

BERRIES SPINACH MIX SMOOTHIE

Calories: 800cal.

Prep Time: 5 mins.
Cook Time: 3 mins.

INGREDIENTS:

- ☐ 1 cup frozen blueberries.
- ☐ 1 cup frozen strawberries.
- ☐ 1 cup baby spinach.

- ☐ 2 tbsps honey or maple syrup.
- ☐ 2 tbsps nut butter (peanut or almond).
- ☐ 3 tbsps hulled hemp seeds.
- ☐ ¼-½ inch fresh ginger, peeled and roughly chopped.
- ☐ ¼-½ cup rolled oats.
- ☐ ¼ cup full fat yogurt or whole milk or ½ a medium banana.
- ☐ 1 cup water.

NOTE: the 800cal count is based on the smaller measurements where you have options, so free to go with the smaller ones or above.

DIRECTIONS:

Add all ingredients to a high-powered blender and blend until creamy. Feel free to add more milk if it is too thick.

BANANA CINNAMON OATMEAL SMOOTHIE

Calories: 800cal.

Prep Time: 4 mins.

Cook Time: 3 mins.

INGREDIENTS:

- 1 cup whole milk.
- ½ cup rolled oats.
- 1 large banana.
- 2 tbsps nut butter.
- ¼ cup full-fat Greek yogurt.
- 1 tsp vanilla extract.
- 1-2 tsp cinnamon.
- 1 ¼ tbsp ground chia or flax seeds.
- 1 ½ tbsp honey or maple syrup.
- Ice cubes.

DIRECTIONS:

Add all ingredients to a high-powered blender and blend until creamy. Feel free to add more milk if it is too thick or more ice, if too thin.

NOTE:

Include smoothie recipes you enjoyed last week to have more options.

WEEK 2 MAIN RECIPES

RICE AND BEANS

Calories: 1,600cal.

Prep Time: 10 mins.
Cook Time: 1hr.

INGREDIENTS:

- ¾ cup beans (black-eyed peas or pinto).
- 1 ½ cups of uncooked rice.
- 1 small onion, *diced*.
- 4 ½ - 5 ½ cups of water.
- Salt to taste.
- ¾ tablespoon butter or coconut oil.

DIRECTIONS:

- Soak the beans in enough water to totally submerge it. and leave it for a minimum of 3 hours on the countertop or leave it overnight in the Fridge, to reduce its gas producing properties.
- Rinse the beans and transfer it to a pot. Add the diced onion and water, and leave it to cook for about 40 to 50 minutes or till you can easily crush it with your finger.
- Rinse the rice thoroughly until the water comes out clear, stir in the rice, butter/oil, and salt with the beans. Add water if necessary.
- Return to a boil, reduce heat to medium-low, cover and cook for 20 minutes without removing the lid.
- Fold the rice and beans together gently and serve with your desired sauce, soup, or stew. Top with grilled chicken, turkey or beef.

This recipe is for two portions, so divide into two parts, eat one and refrigerate the leftover in a sealed container for the next day or freeze.

PAN FRIED PEPPERONI PIZZA

Calories: 1,630cal.

Prep Time: 10 mins.

Cook Time: 25 mins.

INGREDIENTS:
- 6 large eggs.
- 6 tbsps grated parmesan cheese.
- 3 tbsps psyllium husk powder.
- 3 tbsps olive oil.
- 1 ½ tsp Italian seasoning.
- 9 tbsps tomato sauce, divided.
- 4 ½ ounces shredded mozzarella, divided.
- 1 ½ ounces diced pepperoni, divided.
- 3 tbsps fresh chopped basil.
- Salt.

DIRECTIONS:
- Combine the eggs, parmesan cheese, psyllium husk powder, Italian seasoning and a pinch of salt in a blender. Blend until smooth and well combined, about 35 seconds, then let rest for 5 mins. Divide batter into four portions.
- Heat 1 tbsp of oil in a skillet over medium- high heat.
- Spoon ⅓ of the butter into the skillet and spread in a circle, add one portion of the blended mixture and cook until browned underneath.
- Flip the pizza crust and cook until browned on the other side.
- Move the crust to a foil-lined baking sheet, and repeat steps with the remaining batter portions.
- Spoon 2 ¼ tbsps of tomato sauce over each crust.

- Top with diced pepperoni and shredded cheese
- Sprinkle with fresh basil, and slice pizza to serve.

This recipe is for two portions, so divide into two parts, eat one and refrigerate the leftover in a sealed container for the next day or freeze.

ASSORTED YOGURT GRANOLA BOWL

Calories: 835cal.

Prep Time: 5 mins.
Cook Time: none.

INGREDIENTS:
- 1 - 1 ½ cup full-fat Greek yogurt.
- 2 tbsps chia seeds or 1 tbsp chia, 1 tbsp flax.
- 2 tbsps nut butter (peanut or almond).
- 1 medium banana, chopped.
- ½ cup strawberries.
- ½ pear, chopped or nectarine wedges.

- 4 tbsps granola.

- 1-2 tbsps honey.
- 1 tbsp shredded coconut.

DIRECTIONS:
- Scoop yogurt into a bowl and top with toppings.

CHICKEN QUESADILLA

Calories: 744cal.

Prep Time: 10 mins.
Cook Time: 20 mins.

INGREDIENTS:
- 2 flour tortillas.
- ½ lb chicken breast, cut into smaller pieces.
- ½ tbsp oil.
- ¾ cup Mexican cheese.
- ½ tbsp taco seasoning.
- ¾ tbsp butter.

- ¼ yellow onion, diced.
- ¼ large bell pepper, any color, diced.

DIRECTIONS:

- Preheat a skillet with oil on medium heat. Add in chicken and taco seasoning. Cook for 4 minutes.
- Add in bell pepper and onion, cook for another 5 minutes or until chicken and veggies gain color. Set aside.
- On a clean skillet, add a bit of butter and place a tortilla on top. On half of the tortilla add cheese, the chicken mixture, and cover with more cheese. Fold the tortilla over to close.
- Once the tortilla is golden, flip it over and cook for a few more minutes until that side is golden also. Make sure the cheese has melted. Repeat the same steps with the second tortilla.
- Serve warm.

SPAGHETTI WITH BEEF SAUCE

Calories: 1,944cal.

Prep Time: 5 mins.

Cook Time: 40 mins.

INGREDIENTS:

- 0.75 pound lean ground meat like beef, turkey, chicken or lamb.
- 2 tbsps olive oil.
- ¾ cup chopped onion.
- 2 garlic cloves, minced.
- 1 ¼ tbsps tomato paste.
- ¼ teaspoon dried oregano.
- Pinch crushed red pepper flakes.
- ¾ cup water, broth or dry red wine.
- ¾ (28-ounce) can crushed tomatoes.
- Salt and black pepper.
- Handful fresh basil leaves, plus more for serving.
- 8 ounces dried spaghetti.
- ¼ cup shredded parmesan cheese.

Optional:

- 2 teaspoons fish sauce.
- 2 anchovy filets, minced with some of their oil or use anchovy paste.
- Pinch sugar.
- 1 leftover rind from a wedge of parmesan.

DIRECTIONS:

For the sauce:

- Heat the oil in a large pot over medium-high heat. Add the meat and cook until browned, about 8 minutes.

- As the meat cooks, use a wooden spoon to break it up into smaller crumbles.
- Add the onions and cook, stirring every once and a while, until softened, about 5 minutes.
- Stir in the garlic, tomato paste, oregano, and red pepper flakes and cook, stirring continuously for about 1 minute.
- Pour in the water and use a wooden spoon to scrape up any bits of meat or onion stuck to the bottom of the pot. Stir in the tomatoes, 3/4 teaspoon of salt, and a generous pinch of black pepper.
- Bring the sauce to a low simmer. Cook, uncovered, at a low simmer for 25 minutes. As it cooks, stir and taste the sauce a few times so you can adjust the seasoning accordingly.

Cook spaghetti:

- About 15 minutes before the sauce finishes cooking, bring a large pot of salted water to the boil, and then cook pasta according to package directions, but check for doneness a minute or two before the suggested cooking time.

Finishing:

- Take the sauce off of the heat, and then stir in the basil. Toss in the cooked pasta, and then leave for a minute so that the pasta absorbs some of the sauce. Toss again, and then serve with parmesan sprinkled on top.

This recipe is for two portions, so divide into two parts, eat one and refrigerate the leftover in a sealed container for the next day or freeze.

NOTE:

✓If the sauce tastes light on flavor, think about adding a few dashes of fish sauce or a few minced anchovies or anchovy paste (both add a rich, savory flavor).

✓If the sauce is too acidic, a pinch of sugar will do the trick.

✓The meat sauce can be made in advance and should last in your refrigerator for up to 3 days and in your freezer for about three months.

✓If the flavor of the sauce doesn't pop, you probably need a bit more salt.

BANANA CHOCOLATE CHIP OATMEAL

Calories: 685cal.

Prep Time: 3 mins.
Cook Time: 4 mins.

INGREDIENTS:

- ½ cup oats.
- ½ cup whole milk.
- ¼ cup full-fat Greek yogurt.
- 1 tbsp chia seeds.

- 1-2 tbsps honey or maple syrup.
- ¼ tsp vanilla extract.
- ½ large banana or 1 medium, sliced.
- 1 tbsp nutella or peanut butter.
- 1 tbsp crushed hazelnuts or peanuts.
- 1-2 tbsp chocolate chips.

DIRECTIONS:

- Bring the cup of milk, sweetener of choice and vanilla extract to a boil in a small saucepan.
- Stir oats and reduce heat to medium; cook for 1 minute.
- Remove from heat and let stand for 2 minutes to cool off.
- Add yogurt, chia seeds, sliced banana, nutella or nut butter, crushed nuts, and chocolate chips as toppings.

BONUS SNACK RECIPE

CHOCOLATE CHIP MUFFINS

Calories: 384cal per serving.

Prep Time: 10 mins.
Cook Time: 20 mins.
Servings: 12.

INGREDIENTS:

- 2 large eggs.
- 3/4 cup sour cream (170g).
- 1/2 cup whole milk (120ml).
- 2 teaspoons vanilla extract (10ml).
- 1-3/4 cups all-purpose flour (210g).
- 2/3 cup unsweetened cocoa powder (60g).
- 1 cup granulated sugar (200g).
- 1 1/2 teaspoons baking powder.
- 1 teaspoon baking soda.
- 3/4 teaspoon salt.
- 2 cups of chocolate chips.
- 1/2 cup vegetable oil (120ml).

DIRECTIONS:

- Preheat the oven to 425F and line a muffin tin with paper.
- Sift the flour, cocoa powder, baking soda, baking powder, salt, and sugar into a large bowl. Whisk together and set aside.
- In a separate bowl combine the eggs, vanilla, vegetable oil, sour cream, and milk then whisk together.
- Set aside about 1/3 cup of the chocolate chips for the muffin tops.

- Pour the wet into the dry and fold together using a spatula, mixing until almost combined. Sprinkle in the remaining chocolate chips and mix until the batter is just combined and the chocolate chips have been distributed.
- Fill the muffin papers to the top and sprinkle with the reserved chocolate chips. Bake at 425F for 6 minutes then reduce to 350F and continue baking for about 14 minutes or until the centers are set, a toothpick or skewer inserted in the center will come out clean.

NOTE:
- Don't open the oven door or you risk the muffins deflating!
- You can easily change up the flavors by adding in orange zest or even peppermint extract for a mint choc version.
- Feel free to switch the chocolate chips for your favorites. You could use white chocolate or butterscotch chips too.
- The muffins will keep well for up to 3-5 days in an airtight container or can be frozen for up to 3 months.

WEEK 2 GROCERY LIST

VEGETABLE	MISC	DAIRY	BAKING
Corn: as desired	Rice: 2 ½ cups, raw	Butter: 10 tbsps	All-purpose flour: ¾ cup
Carrots: 1 ½, medium	Spaghetti: 8 ounces	Milk: 3 ½ cups, whole milk	Sugar
Onions: 2, small	Bread: 12 slices	Mayonnaise: 4 tbsps	Baking powder
Green onions: 5	Oats: 1 ½ cup, rolled oats	Greek yogurt: 3 ½ cups	Chocolate chips: ½ cup
Garlic: 5 cloves	Sweet Potatoes: 1.25lbs	Cheese of choice for sandwiches: 4 tbsps, grated	Vanilla extract
Bell peppers: 3-4, preferred colors	Peanut or almond butter: 11 tbsps	Mexican cheese: ¾ cup	Maple syrup
Basil: 3 tbsps, chopped, 1-2 handfuls	Olive oil	Parmesan cheese: 6 tbsps, grated, ¼ cup shredded	Shredded coconut: 2 tbsps
Yellow onion: 1, small	Chia seeds: 5 tbsps		Cinnamon
	Tomato sauce: 9 tbsps	**MISC**	Honey

Peas: ¼ cup	Shredded mozzarella: 4 ½ ounces	Soy sauce	Granola: 8 tbsps
Parsley, cilantro: as desired	Taco seasoning: ½ tbsp	Toasted sesame oil	Flour tortillas: 4
	Thyme powder	Cayenne pepper	Crushed peanuts or hazelnuts
	Tomato paste: 2 tbsps	Black pepper	
	28 oz can crushed tomatoes		
	Black-eyed peas or pinto beans: ¾ cup		

FRUITS	PROTEIN	MISC
Apples: 2, medium	Eggs: 17, large	Salt
Bananas: 6, medium	Chicken: 4oz	Psyllium husk powder: 3 tbsps
Strawberries: 1 ½ cups	Chicken: ¾ cup shredded, ½ lb ground	Italian seasoning
Pear: 1	Diced pepperoni: 1 ½ ounces	Smoked paprika
	Lean ground meat like beef, turkey or chicken: 0.75lb	

- ☐ Include the ingredients of your chosen smoothies for the week (just double or triple the ingredients). Remember to include your protein powder if you use them.
- ☐ Don't forget to include your snacks if you're getting any.

WEEK 3

	BREAKFAST	LUNCH
SUNDAY	English breakfast + 1 cup of whole milk Calories: 900cal	1st portion of easy beef curry Calories: 820cal
MONDAY	Assorted yogurt granola bowl Calories: 835cal	Mayo chicken sandwich Calories: 770cal
TUESDAY	Baked eggs in avocado with bacon and toast + 1 cup of whole milk Calories: 770cal	Leftover fried spaghetti Calories: 765cal
WEDNESDAY	Peanut butter and banana sandwich: 2 slices bread toast, 4 tbsp peanut butter, 1 medium banana, 1 cup whole milk Calories: 756cal	1st portion of easy mushroom risotto Calories: 825cal
THURSDAY	English breakfast + 1 cup of whole milk Calories: 900cal	Crispy chipotle chicken thighs Calories: 800cal
FRIDAY	Omelet: 2 large eggs, 1 tbsp butter, 2 tbsp grated cheese, cherry tomatoes, herbs and spices of choice.	Chicken sweet potatoes hash Calories: 820cal

	Oatmeal: ½ cup raw quick oats, 1 cup whole milk, 1 medium apple, cinnamon, sweetener of choice. <u>Calories: 780cal</u>	
SATURDAY	Cottage cheese pancakes with jelly <u>Calories: 910cal</u>	Bacon egg bombs <u>Calories: 800cal</u>

	DINNER	**SMOOTHIE**	**TOTAL CALORIES**
SUNDAY	1st portion of fried spaghetti <u>Calories: 765cal</u>	✓	3,285 cal.
MONDAY	Leftover easy beef curry <u>Calories: 820cal</u>	✓	3,225 cal.
TUESDAY	Oven-roasted sweet potatoes <u>Calories: 800cal</u>	✓	3,135 cal.
WEDNESDAY	Bacon egg bombs <u>Calories: 800cal</u>	✓	3,181 cal.
THURSDAY	Leftover easy mushroom risotto <u>Calories: 825cal</u>	✓	3,325 cal.
FRIDAY	Assorted yogurt granola bowl <u>Calories: 835cal</u>	✓	3,235 cal.
SATURDAY	Peanut butter and strawberry jelly oatmeal <u>Calories: 710cal</u>	✓	3,220 cal.

WEEK 3 SMOOTHIE RECIPES

ORANGE PINEAPPLE SMOOTHIE

Calories: 876cal.

Prep Time: 4 mins.
Cook Time: 3 mins.

INGREDIENTS:
- 1 ½ cups orange juice.
- 3 cups pineapple chunks packed in juice and drained.
- 1 ½ medium banana.
- ½ cup whole milk.
- 3 tbsps honey.
- 5-7 ice cubes.

DIRECTIONS:

- Place all ingredients in a high-powered blender and blend until smooth.

BANANA WALNUT SMOOTHIE

Calories: 800cal.

Prep Time: 4 mins.
Cook Time: 3 mins.

INGREDIENTS:

- 2 cups whole milk.
- ⅓ cup walnuts, unshelled.
- 2 medium frozen bananas.
- 2 Medjool dates soaked for 10 minutes.
- ¼ tsp cinnamon (optional).

DIRECTIONS:

- Add all the ingredients to your high-powered blender and process until smooth.

PEANUT BUTTER AND BERRIES PROTEIN SMOOTHIE

Calories: 810cal.

Prep Time: 3 mins.
Cook Time: 3 mins.

INGREDIENTS:
- 1 ½ medium banana, frozen.
- 1 cup full-fat Greek yogurt.
- ½ cup frozen strawberries.
- ½ cup frozen blueberries.
- 1 cup whole milk.
- 2 tbsps peanut butter.
- 1 tbsp honey.

DIRECTIONS:
- Add all the ingredients to your high-powered blender and process until smooth.

NOTE: **Include smoothie recipes you enjoyed from the past two weeks to have more options.**

WEEK 3 MAIN MEALS

ENGLISH BREAKFAST

Calories: 760cal.

Prep Time: 6 mins.
Cook Time: 25 mins.

INGREDIENTS:

- ½ can beans, Heinz preferred.
- 2 links breakfast sausages.
- 2 slices back bacon or Irish bacon.
- ½ cup mushrooms halved or sliced.
- 1 small tomato, halved.
- 2 slices of bread.
- 2 eggs, large.
- 2 slices black pudding (optional).
- Salt and pepper.
- Butter or oil.

DIRECTIONS:

- Heat up the beans over low heat in a small pot. Keep warm on low heat.
- Cook the sausages over low to medium heat, turning occasionally, until brown and cooked through. In the same pan, cook the bacon, flipping as needed. Fry the blood pudding slices over medium heat for 3-4 minutes per side.
- In another pan, heat up a bit of oil and cook the mushrooms, without moving, until brown and caramelized. Remove from the pan, then sear the cut side of the tomato briefly. Remove from the pan and season everything with salt and pepper.
- Wipe the pan down and heat up a bit of oil or butter over medium heat. Fry the bread until golden, flipping and adding more oil or butter as needed. Remove and set aside. Finally, fry the eggs to your liking. Plate everything up: sausages, bacon, black pudding, mushrooms, tomato, bread, and eggs. Enjoy!

EASY BEEF CURRY

Calories: 1,640cal.

Prep Time: 20 mins.

Cook Time: 40 mins.

INGREDIENTS:

- 1 medium yellow onion, chopped.
- 1 tbsp grated ginger.
- 1 tbsp minced garlic.
- 1 ¼ cups canned coconut milk.
- 2 tbsps curry powder.
- 1 lb beef chuck, chopped.
- Salt to taste.
- ½ cup fresh chopped cilantro.
- Seasoning cube (optional).

DIRECTIONS:

- Combine the onion, garlic and ginger in a food processor and blend into a paste.
- Transfer the paste to a saucepan and cook on medium heat for 3 minutes.
- Stir in the coconut milk and simmer gently for 10 minutes.
- Add the chopped beef along with salt and the curry powder.
- Stir well, cover it and let it simmer for 20 minutes.
- Remove the lid and simmer for another 20 minutes until the beef is cooked through.
- Adjust seasoning to taste and garnish with fresh chopped cilantro.

This recipe is for two portions, so divide into two parts, eat one and refrigerate the leftover in a sealed container for the next day or freeze.

BAKED EGGS IN AVOCADO WITH BACON AND TOAST

Calories: 630cal.

Prep Time: 5 mins.
Cook Time: 25 mins.

INGREDIENTS:

- 1 large avocado.
- 2 medium sized eggs.
- 2 slices bacon , cooked then crumbled.
- 2 slices of toast.
- Salt to taste.
- Black pepper to taste.
- Hot sauce (optional).
- Fresh chopped tomatoes (optional).

DIRECTIONS:

- Preheat the oven to 425°F.
- Crack the eggs in individual bowls, careful to not puncture the yolks. Set aside. You can crack the egg directly in the avocado later, but it might overflow and make a mess.

- Cut avocado in half and carefully remove seed. Depending on how big the seed is, the hole in the avocado should be big enough for one small egg. But if the hole looks too small, scoop out a little at a time until it matches the amount of egg.
- Make aluminum foil rings to hold the avocados level. You need to keep the avocado from tilting so that the raw egg does not spill over. In a medium sized baking dish, lay a foil ring, and rest the avocado half on top so that the avocado doesn't tilt over. Press down on foil if needed to align the avocado.
- Carefully place the eggs into the avocado seed cavities ~ If you aren't sure if the cavity is big enough to hold all the egg whites, this technique will be useful: With a spoon, gently scoop out one of the yolks and place it into the hole of the avocado. Then continue spooning the egg whites into the avocado hole until it's full. Repeat for the other avocado half.
- Add salt and fresh cracked black pepper on top of the eggs, to taste.
- Carefully place the baking dish in the oven and bake for about 15-30 minutes, or until the eggs are cooked to your preference. Keep checking the egg to see if it's cooked to your desired consistency. Bake them for less time if you like runny egg yolks.
- Sprinkle crumbled bacon on top. Spread the avocado/egg on toast. Add additional salt and pepper to taste, chopped tomatoes, hot sauce, if needed.

EASY MUSHROOM RISOTTO

Calories: 1,650cal.

Prep Time: 10 mins.
Cook Time: 20 mins.

INGREDIENTS:

- 3 tablespoons butter.
- 1 ½ medium onion, finely diced.
- 3 cloves garlic, finely minced or pressed.
- 1 ½ tablespoons fresh lemon juice.
- 1 ½ teaspoon chopped fresh thyme (dried thyme also works).
- 1 ½ - 3 pinches of salt and pepper.
- ¼ - ½ cup white wine.
- 1 ½ cups of arborio rice (also called risotto rice).
- 2 ¼ cups chopped white mushrooms.
- 6 cups of hot chicken or vegetable stock.
- Fresh parsley or thyme and Parmesan cheese to garnish.

DIRECTIONS:

- Heat a large skillet over medium heat and add the butter.
- Once the butter is melted, add the onion and garlic and sauté until the onion is soft and translucent.
- Add the lemon juice, thyme and salt and pepper.
- Add the wine and stir as the wine reduces (cook for about 5 minutes until the wine reduces).
- Turn the heat to medium-low and add the rice. Toss the rice in the onion mixture until it's coated and move it around the pan for about 1 minute.
- Stir in the mushrooms.
- Add the hot chicken stock (or vegetable stock) about 1/2 cup at a time, stirring constantly and waiting until the stock is absorbed by the rice until you add another 1/2 cup.
- Repeat the process above until all the stock has been added and absorbed by the rice and a creamy sauce has formed, stirring constantly throughout.
- Serve immediately with shaved Parmesan cheese and freshly chopped thyme or parsley.

This recipe is for two portions, so divide into two parts, eat one and refrigerate the leftover in a sealed container for the next day or freeze.

CRISPY CHIPOTLE CHICKEN THIGHS

Calories: 800cal.

Prep Time: 15 mins.
Cook Time: 15 mins.

INGREDIENTS:

- ½ tsp chipotle chili powder.
- ¼ tsp garlic powder.
- ¼ tsp onion powder.
- ¼ tsp smoked paprika.
- ¼ tsp ground coriander.
- 12 ounces boneless chicken thighs.
- 1 tbsp olive oil.
- 3 cups of fresh baby spinach.
- Salt and pepper.

DIRECTIONS:

- Combine the chipotle chili powder, garlic powder, onion powder, ground coriander and smoked paprika in a bowl.
- Lay chicken thighs flat and season with salt and pepper on both sides.
- Cut the chicken thighs in half, then heat oil in a skillet over medium-high heat.

- Add the chicken thighs skin-side-down to the skillet and sprinkle with the spice mixture. Cook for 8 mins, then flip to the other side, sprinkle spice mixture and cook for 5 mins.
- Add spinach to the skillet during the last 3-4 mins and cook till wilted.
- Serve crispy chicken thighs on a bed of wilted spinach.

COTTAGE CHEESE PANCAKES WITH JELLY

Calories: 910cal.

Prep Time: 7 mins.
Cook Time: 15 mins.

INGREDIENTS:

- ½ cup cottage cheese.
- 2 medium eggs, lightly beaten.
- 6 tbsps all-purpose flour.
- ¾ cup whole milk.
- 1 tbsp coconut oil.
- 2 tbsps butter.

- 2-3 tbsps full-fat Greek yogurt.
- 2 tbsps honey.
- 2-3 tbsps raspberry or strawberry jelly.

DIRECTIONS:

- Mix cottage cheese, flour, coconut oil, eggs, milk, and honey in a bowl or blend everything up.
- Add butter to a skillet and add a ladle of the pancake batter.
- Flip after 2 minutes.
- Serve pancakes hot with a dollop of Greek yogurt and jelly.

BACON EGG BOMBS

Calories: 800cal.

Prep Time: 40 mins.
Cook Time: none.

INGREDIENTS:

- 3 slices thick-cut bacon.

- 2 large eggs.
- 3 tbsps butter.
- 1 ½ tbsps mayonnaise.
- Salt and pepper to taste.

DIRECTIONS:

- Cook the bacon in a skillet over medium-high heat until crisp.
- Let the bacon cool a little, chop it up and set aside, reserving the bacon grease.
- Fill a saucepan with water, add 1-2 pinches of salt and bring to a boil.
- Add the eggs and boil them for 10 minutes. Transfer to a bowl with water to cool. After cooling, peel off the shells and chop them coarsely.
- Mash the chopped eggs with the butter , then stir in the mayonnaise, salt, and pepper.
- Stir in the reserved bacon grease, then cover the mixture and chill for 30 minutes.
- Divide the egg mixture into 6-8 portions, roll them into balls, add in the crushed bacon. Serve immediately.

BONUS SNACK RECIPE

OATMEAL COOKIES

Calories: 125cal per serving.

Prep Time: 15 mins.
Cook Time: 30 mins.
Servings: 20.

INGREDIENTS:

- ☐ 1 cup all-purpose flour, spooned and leveled.
- ☐ ½ teaspoon baking soda.
- ☐ ½ teaspoon baking powder.
- ☐ ½ teaspoon sea salt.
- ☐ ½ teaspoon cinnamon.
- ☐ ½ cup coconut oil or butter, melted.
- ☐ ¾ cup brown sugar.
- ☐ 1 large egg.
- ☐ 1 large egg yolk.
- ☐ 2 teaspoons vanilla extract.

- 1 ½ cup rolled oats.
- ¾ cup raisins, dried cranberries or chocolate chips.
- ½ cup chopped walnuts (optional).

DIRECTIONS:

- Preheat the oven to 350°F and line two baking sheets with parchment paper.
- Combine the flour, baking soda, baking powder, salt, and cinnamon in a large bowl. In a separate bowl, whisk together the melted coconut oil, sugar, whole egg, egg yolk, and vanilla, whisking vigorously.
- Stir the wet ingredients into the dry ingredients. Stir in the oats, raisins or preferred other and walnuts, if using, folding into a tight batter. Set the dough aside for 20 minutes while the oven preheats. (Note: if your dough seems too wet to become scoop-able, chill it in the fridge for 20 minutes and it'll firm up). If your dough is too crumbly, stir in 2 to 3 tablespoons of water.
- Scoop into 20 tablespoon-sized balls and roll lightly in barely damp hands to make them round. Spread out onto the prepared baking sheets and bake until puffed, golden, and a touch underbaked-looking, 10 to 11 minutes. Let cool on the pans for 5 minutes before transferring to a wire rack to cool completely.

WEEK 3 GROCERY LIST

VEGETABLE	MISC	DAIRY	BAKING
Fresh baby spinach: 3 cups	Salt	Cheese of your choice for omelet: 2 tbsps, grated	All-purpose flour: 6 tbsps
Garlic: 4 cloves, 2 tbsps minced	Pepper	Butter: 13 tbsps	Coconut oil
Onion: 3 ½, medium	Strawberry or raspberry jelly	Mayonnaise: 6 tbsps	Granola: 8 tbsps
Fresh or dried thyme: as desired	Garlic powder	Cottage cheese: ½ cup	Cinnamon
Parsley: as desired	Onion powder	Whole milk: 7 cups	Honey
Fresh cilantro: ½ cup	Smoked paprika	Full-fat Greek yogurt: 4 cups	Chia seeds: 5 tbsps
Ginger: 1 tbsp, grated	Ground coriander		Shredded coconut: 2 tbsps
Yellow onion: 1, medium	Chipotle chili powder		Vanilla extract
Tomatoes: 2	White wine: ¼-½ cup	**MISC**	
Bell peppers: 1 ½ cups, mixed	Risotto rice: 1 ½ cups	Sweet Potatoes: 3.25 pounds	

Green onions: 2 tbsps, sliced	Chicken or vegetable stock: 6 cups	Spaghetti: 250g	
Mixed vegetables: ¾ cup (peas, corn, cucumber)	Canned coconut milk: 1 ¼ cups		
Spring onions: 2	Bread: 11 slices		
	Curry powder		
	Heinz beans: 1 can		

FRUITS	PROTEIN	MISC
Fresh lemon juice	Thick-cut bacon: 8 slices Back bacon: 4 slices	Oats: 1 cup, rolled
Avocado: 1, large	Eggs: 14, large	Peanut butter: 10 tbsps
Bananas: 3, medium	12 oz, boneless chicken thighs	Peanuts
Pear: 1	White mushrooms: 4 ¼ cups	Cayenne pepper
Strawberries: 1 ¼ cups	Beef chuck: 1 lb	Soy sauce
Apple: 1, medium	Breakfast sausage: 4 links	Seasoning cube: 1
	Chicken: ¾ cup, shredded ½ lb, ground	
	Shrimp: 150g	

Include the ingredients of your chosen smoothies for the week (just double or triple the ingredients). Remember to include your protein powder if you use them. Don't forget to include snacks if you're getting any.

NOTE

- Adding glasses of juice to your meals will boost your calories.
- Have your roasted sweet potatoes with sauce.
- Feel free to add as many condiments to your food as you would like, such as adding extra butter, cream, oils, cheese, whole milk, whipped cream, mayonnaise, salad dressing, jelly, jam, syrup, and honey.
- Avoid drinking beverages with meals. These take up room in your stomach, making you feel full faster. Save them for in-between meals.
- Avoid foods labeled "lite" or "diet".
- Feel free to add avocado to your omelet and grilled chicken sandwich for extra calories.
- If you're replacing whole milk with non-dairy milk, add tablespoons of nuts to that meal as a snack. If in smoothies, add toppings in the form of nuts, seeds, raisins, shredded coconut and chocolate chips to makeup for the reduced calorie count.
- Feel free to replace nuts with your favorite seeds, and peanut butter with other nut butters.
- Butter may be replaced with coconut oil or nut butter of choice depending on the recipe.
- Rice can be replaced with quinoa in equal measurements.

- Granola bars included are calculated as being 250 calories. So make sure to remember to check the calorie content when buying granola bars during your grocery shoppings.
- Calorie counts are not 100% accurate due to differences in brand of products and measurement differences.
- For recipes containing non-fat Greek yogurt yogurt, feel free to replace non-fat Greek yogurt with full-fat Greek yogurt.
- Replace chicken in sandwiches with equal measurements for turkey and double the measurements for tuna.
- Remember to take a smoothie daily as a snack, at your preferred time.
- You can make batches of bonus snacks during the weekend and eat them throughout the new week.
- Have nuts, seeds or dried fruits with you always for easy snacking.

SNACK SUGGESTIONS

- Handful of nuts such as cashews, pecans, peanuts, walnuts, almonds with or without dried fruits like dates, raisins and seeds like pumpkin, flax, chia. (trail mix).
- Yogurt, granola and fruit parfaits.
- Fruit and vegetable salads.
- Granola and chocolate bars.
- Crackers and cheese or dips.
- Chips, popcorn.
- Chocolate chip cookies.
- Bread buns.
- Full-fat Greek yogurt.
- Dried figs and apricots, prunes, Medjool dates.
- Nut butter and jelly sandwich.
- Chocolate milk cartons.
- Cereals, weetabix.
- Celery stalks, nut butter and raisins.
- High calorie liquid nutritional supplement such as ensure.
- Ice cream.
- Wafers.
- Instant noodles.

- ☐ Hot chocolate.
- ☐ Biscuits.
- ☐ Roasted corn.
- ☐ Coconut flakes.
- ☐ Rice crispy bites.
- ☐ Hummus.
- ☐ Boiled eggs with spices and seasonings.
- ☐ Homemade fruit juices.
- ☐ Glasses of milk.
- ☐ Homemade muffins.
- ☐ Oatmeal bars and cookies.
- ☐ Pear crisps.
- ☐ Puddings.
- ☐ Cottage cheese cups.
- ☐ Beef sticks, beef jerky.
- ☐ Whole wheat pretzels.
- ☐ Fruits and nut butters.
- ☐ Crackers with nut butters.
- ☐ Egg salads.
- ☐ Dark chocolate.
- ☐ Fried chicken.
- ☐ Sardines.

FROM THE AUTHOR

Dear readers,

Thank you so much for being part of my weight gain community! I hope you like this meal plan and enjoy these recipes.

Weight gaining is hard enough without having to consume bland foods. My goal is to provide you with easy and versatile recipes that taste good, as well as an easy to follow meal plan. Feel free to tweak recipes and switch meals, as long as you're getting your daily required calories.

If you have any questions or suggestions you'd like to see me implement, feel free to email me at pharmbtdavies@gmail.com.
I respond to messages everyday.

Barbara.

Made in the USA
Coppell, TX
07 June 2023

17804041R00050